POWER & WEALTH

T0144935

POWER & WEALTH

by Ralph Waldo Emerson

*The Immortal Classics on
Will & Money—
Now in Special Condensations*

Abridged and Introduced
by Mitch Horowitz

THE CONDENSED CLASSICS LIBRARY™

MEDIA

Published by Gildan Media LLC
aka G&D Media.
www.GandDmedia.com

Power and *Wealth* were first published in Ralph Waldo Emerson's
collection *The Conduct of Life* in 1860
G&D Media Condensed Classics edition published 2019
Abridgement and Introduction copyright © 2019 by Mitch
Horowitz

FIRST PRINT AND EBOOK EDITION: 2019

Cover design by David Rheinhardt of Pyrographx

Interior design by Meghan Day Healey of Story Horse, LLC.

ISBN: 978-1-7225-0198-3

Contents

Genius and Practicality
By Mitch Horowitz

Part of Ralph Waldo Emerson's greatness as a writer is that he never shied away from practicality. This was true of his philosophical descendant William James, as well. It can be argued that Emerson's most practical works—which include his essays *Power* and *Wealth*—were not among his greatest. Critic Irving Howe wrote that in such works the philosopher "merely tugs the complexities . . . into the shallows of the explicit."

There is truth in this charge. And yet this judgment fails to take account of Emerson's bravery. Emerson felt obligated to be direct—to provide his readers with plans of action. If this approach reduced philosophical heights, it also banished authorial cowardice. Emerson would not dodge the question of *how* to practice the kinds of self-driven living that his philosophical essays endorsed.

Hence, it is in his essays *Power* and *Wealth*, which Emerson published in *The Conduct of Life* in 1860, that the Transcendentalist prescribed exactly how and under what conditions a person can successfully assert his will in outer life.

In *Power*, Emerson names four essential elements to exercising personal power. The first—and that which sustains all the others—is to be "in sympathy with the course of things." Displaying his innate instinct for Taoism and other Eastern philosophies, Emerson believed that an individual could read the *nature of things* and seek to merge with it, like a twig carried downstream. "The mind that is parallel with the laws of nature," he writes, "will be in the current of events, and strong with their strength."

The second element of power is *health*. Emerson means this on different levels. He is speaking broadly of the vitality of body and spirit; the state of physicality and personal morale that sustains risks, seeks adventure, and completes plans. But he also speaks of routine bodily health, without which the individual's energies are sapped.

The third element is *concentration*. One of nature's laws is that concentration of energies brings impact.

The concentration of a striking blow delivers the greatest force. Too often we deplete our energies by dispersing or spreading thin our aims and efforts. In *Power,* an imaginary oracle says: "Enlarge not thy destiny, endeavor not to do more than is given thee in charge." Like light focused in a laser, concentration into a single beam brings the greatest power.

The fourth and final element of power is *drilling.* By this Emerson means repeating a practice over and over until you can perform it with excellence. The martial artist repeats his movements and routines to the point where they enter his physical memory and are available to him under all conditions. Likewise, we must drill— or practice or rehearse—to the point where we have mastered our chosen task.

In the essay *Wealth*, Emerson declares, chin out, that the individual is "born to be rich." And by riches, the philosopher is not employing a coy metaphor. He means cold, hard cash. But he also identifies accumulation of capital as befitting only that person who uses it to productive ends. Emerson writes,

> *Every man is a consumer, and ought to be a producer. He fails to make his place good in the world, unless he not only pays his debt, but also*

adds something to the common wealth. Nor can he do justice to his genius, without making some larger demand on the world than a bare subsistence. He is by constitution expensive, and needs to be rich.

Only those purchases that expand your power and abilities, he writes, leave you any richer. Indeed, wealth that fails to accompany expansion is wealth thrown away. "Nor is the man enriched," Emerson writes, "in repeating the old experiments of animal sensation." Rather, you are enriched when you increase your ability to earn, to do, and to grow. Wealth, properly understood, is power. That is why these essays are conjoined.

So, how do you earn wealth? Emerson outlines roughly three steps: 1) First filling some nonnegotiable, subsistence-level need in your own life: this what drove the primeval farmers, hunter-gathers, and villagers. 2) Next, applying one's particular talents to nature, and expansively filling the needs of others. If you do not know or understand your talents, you must start there before anything is possible. Your particular talent is a source of excellence. And, finally, 3) using your wealth for the purposes of productiveness: paying down debts, making compound investments, and procuring the tools and talents of your trade. Building and expanding is the only sound way to riches. And such things also reflect your code and fiber as a progressing being.

By entering the mechanics of practicality, did Emerson sacrifice some of his transcendental splendor? Some thought so; I see it differently. If Emerson had avoided such an approach he would have been guilty of failing to take his philosophy onto the road. Complexity does not excuse inaction. And here I am reminded of an observation by the flawed and brilliant poet Ezra Pound, to whom I cede the last word: "But to have done instead of not doing/ This is not vanity."

I. Power

Who shall set a limit to the influence of a human being? There are men, who, by their sympathetic attractions, carry nations with them, and lead the activity of the human race. And if there be such a tie, that, wherever the mind of man goes, nature will accompany him, perhaps there are men whose magnetisms are of that force to draw material and elemental powers, and, where they appear, immense instrumentalities organize around them. Life is a search after power; and this is an element with which the world is so saturated,—there is no chink or crevice in which it is not lodged,—that no honest seeking goes unrewarded. A man should prize events and possessions as the ore in which this fine mineral is found; and he can well afford to let events and possessions, and the breath of the body go, if their value has been added to him in the shape of power. If he have secured the elixir, he can spare the wide gardens from which it was distilled. A cultivated man, wise to know and bold to perform, is the end to which nature works, and the education of the will is the flowering and result of all this geology and astronomy.

All successful men have agreed in one thing,— they were *causationists*. They believed that things went not by luck, but by law; that there was not a weak or a cracked link in the chain that joins the first and last of things. A belief in causality, or strict connection between every trifle and the principle of being, and, in consequence, belief in compensation, or, that nothing is got for nothing,—characterizes all valuable minds, and must control every effort that is made by an industrious one. The most valiant men are the best believers in the tension of the laws. "All the great captains," said Bonaparte, "have performed vast achievements by conforming with the rules of the art,—by adjusting efforts to obstacles."

The key to the age may be this, or that, or the other, as the young orators describe; —the key to all ages is— Imbecility; imbecility in the vast majority of men, at all times, and, even in heroes, in all but certain eminent moments; victims of gravity, custom, and fear. This gives force to the strong,—that the multitude have no habit of self-reliance or original action.

We must reckon success a constitutional trait. Courage,—the old physicians taught, (and their meaning holds, if their physiology is a little mythical,)—courage, or the degree of life, is as the degree of circulation of the blood in the arteries. Where the arteries hold their blood, is courage and adventure possible. Where they pour it unrestrained into the veins, the spirit is low and feeble. For performance of great mark, it needs extraordinary health. If Eric is in robust health, and has slept well, and is at the top of his condition, and thirty years old, at his departure from Greenland, he will steer west, and his ships will reach Newfoundland. But take out Eric, and put in a stronger and bolder man,—Biorn, or Thorfin,—and the ships will, with just as much ease, sail six hundred, one thousand, fifteen hundred miles further, and reach Labrador and New England. There is no chance in results. With adults, as with children, one class enter cordially into the game, and whirl with the whirling world; the others have cold hands, and remain bystanders; or are only dragged in by the humor and vivacity of those who can carry a dead weight. The first wealth is health. Sickness is poor-spirited, and cannot serve any one: it must husband its resources to live. But health or fulness answers its own ends, and has to spare, runs over, and inundates the neighborhoods and creeks of other men's necessities.

All power is of one kind, a sharing of the nature of the world. The mind that is parallel with the laws of nature will be in the current of events, and strong with their strength. One man is made of the same stuff of which events are made; is in sympathy with the course of things; can predict it. Whatever befalls, befalls him first; so that he is equal to whatever shall happen. A man who knows men, can talk well on politics, trade, law, war, religion. For, everywhere, men are led in the same manners.

The advantage of a strong pulse is not to be supplied by any labor, art, or concert. It is like the climate, which easily rears a crop, which no glass, or irrigation, or tillage, or manures, can elsewhere rival. It is like the opportunity of a city like New York, or Constantinople, which needs no diplomacy to force capital or genius or labor to it. They come of themselves, as the waters flow to it.

This affirmative force is in one, and is not in another, as one horse has the spring in him, and another in the whip. "On the neck of the young man," said Hafiz, "sparkles no gem so gracious as enterprise." Import into any stationary district, as into an old Dutch population in New York or Pennsylvania, or among the planters of Virginia, a colony of hardy Yankees, with seething brains, heads full of steam-hammer, pulley, crank, and toothed wheel,—and everything begins to shine with values. In every company, there is not only the active and passive sex, but, in both men and women, a deeper and more important *sex of mind*, namely, the inventive or creative class of both men and women, and the uninventive or accepting class. Each plus man represents his set, and, if he have the accidental advantage of personal ascendency,—which implies neither more nor less of talent, but merely the temperamental or taming eye of a soldier or a schoolmaster, (which one has, and one has not, as one has a black moustache and one a blond,) then quite easily and without envy or resistance, all his coadjutors and feeders will admit his right to absorb them.

There is always room for a man of force, and he makes room for many. Society is a troop of thinkers, and the best heads among them take the best places. A feeble man can see the farms that are fenced and tilled, the houses that are built. The strong man sees the possible houses and farms. His eye makes estates, as fast as the sun breeds clouds.

When a new boy comes into school, when a man travels, and encounters strangers every day, or, when into any old club a new comer is domesticated, that happens which befalls, when a strange ox is driven into a pen or pasture where cattle are kept; there is at once a trial of strength between the best pair of horns and the new comer, and it is settled thenceforth which is the leader. So now, there is a measuring of strength, very courteous, but decisive, and an acquiescence thenceforward when these two meet. Each reads his fate in the other's eyes. The weaker party finds, that none of his information or wit quite fits the occasion. He thought he knew this or that: he finds that he omitted to learn the end of it. Nothing that he knows will quite hit the mark, whilst all the rival's arrows are good, and well thrown. But if he knew all the facts in the encyclopaedia, it would not help him: for this is an affair of presence of mind, of attitude, of aplomb: the opponent has the sun and wind, and, in every cast, the choice of weapon and mark; and, when he himself is matched with some other antagonist, his own shafts fly well and hit. 'Tis a question of stomach and constitution. The second man is as good as the first,—perhaps better; but has not stoutness or stomach, as the first has, and so his wit seems over-fine or under-fine.

Health is good,—power, life, that resists disease, poison, and all enemies, and is conservative, as well as creative. Vivacity, leadership, must be had, and we are not allowed to be nice in choosing. And we have a certain instinct, that where is great amount of life, though gross and peccant, it has its own checks and purifications, and will be found at last in harmony with moral laws.

We prosper with such vigor, that, like thrifty trees, which grow in spite of ice, lice, mice, and borers, so we do not suffer from the profligate swarms. The huge animals nourish huge parasites, and the rancor of the disease attests the strength of the constitution.

All kinds of power usually emerge at the same time; good energy, and bad; power of mind, with physical health; the ecstasies of devotion, with the exasperations of debauchery. The same elements are always present, only sometimes these conspicuous, and sometimes those; what was yesterday foreground, being to-day background,—what was surface, playing now a not less effective part as basis. The longer the drought lasts, the more is the atmosphere surcharged with water. The faster the ball falls to the sun, the force to fly off is by so much augmented. And, in morals, wild liberty breeds iron conscience; natures with great impulses have great resources, and return from far. In politics, the sons of democrats will be whigs; whilst red republicanism, in the father, is a spasm of nature to engender an intolerable tyrant in the next age. On the other hand, conservatism, ever more timorous and narrow, disgusts the children, and drives them for a mouthful of fresh air into radicalism.

Those who have most of this coarse energy,—the 'bruisers,' who have run the gauntlet of caucus and tavern through the county or the state, have their own vices, but they have the good nature of strength and courage. Fierce and unscrupulous, they are usually frank and direct, and above falsehood. Our politics fall into bad hands, and churchmen and men of refinement, it seems agreed, are not fit persons to send to Congress. Politics is a deleterious profession, like some poisonous handicrafts. Men in power have no opinions, but may be had cheap for any opinion, for any purpose,—and if it be only a question between the most civil and the most forcible, I lean to the last.

In trade, also, this energy usually carries a trace of ferocity. Philanthropic and religious bodies do not commonly make their executive officers out of saints. The communities hitherto founded by Socialists,—the Jesuits, the Port-Royalists, the American communities at New Harmony, at Brook Farm, at Zoar, are only possible, by installing Judas as steward. The rest of the offices may be filled by good burgesses. The pious and charitable proprietor has a foreman not quite so pious and charitable. The most amiable of country gentle-men has a certain pleasure in the teeth of the bull-dog which guards his orchard. Of the Shaker society, it was formerly a sort of proverb in the country, that they always sent the devil to market. And in representations of the Deity, painting, poetry, and popular religion have ever drawn the wrath from Hell. It is an esoteric doctrine of society, that a little wickedness is good to make muscle; as if conscience were not good for hands and legs, as if poor decayed formalists of law and order cannot run like wild goats, wolves, and conies; that, as there is a use in medicine for poisons, so the world cannot move without rogues; that public spirit and the ready hand are as well found among the malignants. 'Tis not very rare, the coincidence of sharp private and political practice, with public spirit, and good neighborhood.

Whilst thus the energy for originating and executing work, deforms itself by excess, and so our axe chops off our own fingers,—this evil is not without remedy. All the elements whose aid man calls in, will sometimes become his masters, especially those of most subtle force. Shall he, then, renounce steam, fire, and electricity, or, shall he learn to deal with them? The rule for this whole class of agencies is,—all plus is good; only put it in the right place.

Men of this surcharge of arterial blood cannot live on nuts, herb-tea, and elegies; cannot read novels, and play whist; cannot satisfy all their wants at the Thursday Lecture, or the Boston Athenaeum. They pine for adventure, and must go to Pike's Peak; had rather die by the hatchet of a Pawnee, than sit all day and every day at a counting-room desk. They are made for war, for the sea, for mining, hunting, and clearing; for hair-breadth adventures, huge risks, and the joy of eventful living. Some men cannot endure an hour of calm at sea.

The excess of virility has the same importance in general history, as in private and industrial life. Strong race or strong individual rests at last on natural forces, which are best in the savage, who, like the beasts around him, is still in reception of the milk from the teats of Nature. Cut off the connection between any of our works, and this aboriginal source, and the work is shallow. The people lean on this, and the mob is not quite so bad an argument as we sometimes say, for it has this good side. "March without the people," said a French deputy from the tribune, "and you march into night: their instincts are a finger-pointing of Providence, always turned toward real benefit."

The best anecdotes of this force are to be had from savage life, in explorers, soldiers, and buccaneers. But who cares for fallings-out of assassins, and fights of bears, or grindings of icebergs? Physical force has no value, where there is nothing else. Snow in snow-banks, fire in volcanoes and solfataras is cheap. The luxury of ice is in tropical countries, and midsummer days. The luxury of fire is, to have a little on our hearth: and of electricity, not volleys of the charged cloud, but the manageable stream on the battery-wires.

In history, the great moment is, when the savage is just ceasing to be a savage, with all his hairy Pelasgic strength directed on his sense of beauty;—and you have Pericles and Phidias,—not yet passed over into the Corinthian civility. Everything good in nature and the world is in that moment of transition, when the swarthy juices still flow plentifully from nature, but their astringency or acridity is got out by ethics and humanity.

The triumphs of peace have been in some proximity to war. Whilst the hand was still familiar with the sword-hilt, whilst the habits of the camp were still visible in the port and complexion of the gentleman, his intellectual power culminated: the compression and tension of these stern conditions is a training for the finest and softest arts, and can rarely be compensated in tranquil times, except by some analogous vigor drawn from occupations as hardy as war.

We say that success is constitutional; depends on a *plus* condition of mind and body, on power of work, on courage; that it is of main efficacy in carrying on the world, and, though rarely found in the right state for an article of commerce, but oftener in the supersaturate or excess, which makes it dangerous and destructive, yet it cannot be spared, and must be had in that form, and absorbents provided to take off its edge.

The affirmative class monopolize the homage of mankind. They originate and execute all the great feats. What a force was coiled up in the skull of Napoleon! Of the sixty thousand men making his army at Eylau, it seems some thirty thousand were thieves and burglars. The men whom, in peaceful communities, we hold if we can, with iron at their legs, in prisons, under the muskets of sentinels, this man dealt with, hand to hand, dragged them to their duty, and won his victories by their bayonets.

This aboriginal might gives a surprising pleasure when it appears under conditions of supreme refinement, as in the proficients in high art. When Michel Angelo was forced to paint the Sistine Chapel in fresco, of which art he knew nothing, he went down into the Pope's gardens behind the Vatican, and with a shovel dug out ochres, red and yellow, mixed them with glue and water with his own hands, and having, after many trials, at last suited himself, climbed his ladders, and painted away, week after week, month after month, the sibyls and prophets. He surpassed his successors in rough vigor, as much as in purity of intellect and refinement. He was not crushed by his one picture left unfinished at last. Michel was wont to draw his figures first in skeleton, then to clothe them with flesh, and lastly to drape them. "Ah!" said a brave painter to me, thinking on these things, "if a man has failed, you will find he has dreamed instead of working. There is no way to success in our art, but to take off your coat, grind paint, and work like a digger on the railroad, all day and every day."

Success goes thus invariably with a certain *plus* or positive power: an ounce of power must balance an ounce of weight. And, though a man cannot return into his mother's womb, and be born with new amounts of vivacity, yet there are two economies, which are the best *succedanea* which the case admits. The first is, the stopping off decisively our miscellaneous activity, and concentrating our force on one or a few points; as the gardener, by severe pruning, forces the sap of the tree into one or two vigorous limbs, instead of suffering it to spindle into a sheaf of twigs.

"Enlarge not thy destiny," said the oracle: "endeavor not to do more than is given thee in charge." The one prudence in life is concentration; the one evil is dissipation: and it makes no difference whether our dissipations are coarse or fine; property and its cares, friends, and a social habit, or politics, or music, or feasting. Everything is good which takes away one plaything and delusion more, and drives us home to add one stroke of faithful work. Friends, books, pictures, lower duties, talents, flatteries, hopes,—all are distractions which cause oscillations in our giddy balloon, and make a good poise and a straight course impossible. You must elect your work; you shall take what your brain can, and drop all the rest. Only so, can that amount of vital force accumulate, which can make the step from knowing to doing. No matter how much faculty of idle seeing a man has, the step from knowing to doing is rarely taken. 'Tis a step out of a chalk circle of imbecility into fruitfulness. Many an artist lacking this, lacks all: he sees the masculine Angelo or Cellini with despair. He, too, is up to Nature and the First Cause in his thought. But the spasm to collect and swing his whole being into one act, he has not. The poet Campbell said, that "a man accustomed to work was equal to any achievement he resolved on, and, that, for himself, necessity not inspiration was the prompter of his muse."

Concentration is the secret of strength in politics, in war, in trade, in short, in all management of human affairs. One of the high anecdotes of the world is the reply of Newton to the inquiry, "how he had been able to achieve his discoveries?"—"By always intending my mind." Or if you will have a text from politics, take this from Plutarch: "There was, in the whole city, but one street in which Pericles was ever seen, the street which led to the market-place and the council house. He declined all invitations to banquets, and all gay assemblies and company. During the whole period of his administration, he never dined at the table of a friend." Or if we seek an example from trade,—"I hope," said a good man to Rothschild, "your children are not too fond of money and business: I am sure you would not wish that."—"I am sure I should wish that: I wish them to give mind, soul, heart, and body to business,—that is the way to be happy. It requires a great deal of boldness and a great deal of caution, to make a great fortune, and when you have got it, it requires ten times as much wit to keep it. If I were to listen to all the projects proposed to me, I should ruin myself very soon. Stick to one business, young man. Stick to your brewery, and you will be the great brewer of London. Be brewer, and banker, and merchant, and manufacturer, and you will soon be in the Gazette."

Many men are knowing, many are apprehensive and tenacious, but they do not rush to a decision. But in our flowing affairs a decision must be made,—the best, if you can; but any is better than none. There are twenty ways of going to a point, and one is the shortest; but set out at once on one. A man who has that presence of mind which can bring to him on the instant all he knows, is worth for action a dozen men who know as much, but can only bring it to light slowly. The good Speaker in the House is not the man who knows the theory of parliamentary tactics, but the man who decides off-hand. The good judge is not he who does hair-splitting justice to every allegation, but who, aiming at substantial justice, rules something intelligible for the guidance of suitors. The good lawyer is not the man who has an eye to every side and angle of contingency, and qualifies all his qualifications, but who throws himself on your part so heartily, that he can get you out of a scrape. Dr. Johnson said, in one of his flowing sentences, "Miserable beyond all names of wretchedness is that unhappy pair, who are doomed to reduce beforehand to the principles of abstract reason all the details of each domestic day. There are cases where little can be said, and much must be done."

The second substitute for temperament is drill, the power of use and routine. The hack is a better roadster than the Arab barb. In chemistry, the galvanic stream, slow, but continuous, is equal in power to the electric spark, and is, in our arts, a better agent. So in human action, against the spasm of energy, we offset the continuity of drill. We spread the same amount of force over much time, instead of condensing it into a moment. 'Tis the same ounce of gold here in a ball, and there in a leaf. At West Point, Col. Buford, the chief engineer, pounded with a hammer on the trunnions of a cannon, until he broke them off. He fired a piece of ordnance some hundred times in swift succession, until it burst. Now which stroke broke the trunnion? Every stroke. Which blast burst the piece? Every blast. The worst provincial company of actors would go through a play better than the best amateur company. The worst regular troops will beat the best volunteers. Practice is nine tenths. A course of mobs is good practice for orators. All the great speakers were bad speakers at first. Stumping it through England for seven years, made Cobden a consummate debater. Stumping it through New England for twice seven, trained Wendell Phillips. The way to learn German, is, to read the same dozen pages over and over a hundred times, till you know every word and particle in them, and can pronounce and repeat them by heart. No genius can recite a ballad at first reading, so well as mediocrity can at the fifteenth or twentieth reading. A humorous friend of mine thinks, that the reason why Nature is so perfect in her art, and gets up such inconceivably fine sunsets, is, that she has learned how, at last, by dint of doing the same thing so very often. Cannot one converse better on a topic on which he has experience, than on one which is new? Hence the use of drill, and the worthlessness of amateurs to cope with practitioners. Six hours every day at the piano, only to give facility of touch; six hours a day at painting, only to give command of the odious materials, oil, ochres, and brushes. The masters say, that they know a master in music, only by seeing the pose of the hands on the keys;—so difficult and vital an act is the command of the instrument. To have learned the use of the tools, by thousands of manipulations; to have learned the arts of reckoning, by endless adding and dividing, is the power of the mechanic and the clerk.

I remarked in England, in confirmation of a frequent experience at home, that, in literary circles, the men of trust and consideration, bookmakers, editors, university deans and professors, bishops, too, were by no means men of the largest literary talent, but usually of a low and ordinary intellectuality, with a sort of mercantile activity and working talent. Indifferent hacks and mediocrities tower, by pushing their forces to a lucrative point, or by working power, over multitudes of superior men.

I have not forgotten that there are sublime considerations which limit the value of talent and superficial success. We can easily overpraise the vulgar hero. There are sources on which we have not drawn. I know what I abstain from. But this force or spirit, being the means relied on by Nature for bringing the work of the day about,—as far as we attach importance to household life, and the prizes of the world, we must respect that. And I hold, that an economy may be applied to it; it is as much a subject of exact law and arithmetic as fluids and gases are; it may be husbanded, or wasted; every man is efficient only as he is a container or vessel of this force, and never was any signal act or achievement in history, but by this expenditure. This is not gold, but the gold-maker; not the fame, but the exploit.

If these forces and this husbandry are within reach of our will, and the laws of them can be read, we infer that all success, and all conceivable benefit for man, is also, first or last, within his reach, and has its own sublime economies by which it may be attained. The world is mathematical, and has no casualty, in all its vast and flowing curve. Success has no more eccentricity, than the gingham and muslin we weave in our mills. I know no more affecting lesson to our busy, plotting New England brains, than to go into one of the factories with which we have lined all the watercourses in the States. A man hardly knows how much he is a machine, until he begins to make telegraph, loom, press, and locomotive, in his own image. But in these, he is forced to leave out his follies and hindrances, so that when we go to the mill, the machine is more moral than we. Let a man dare go to a loom, and see if he be equal to it. Let machine confront machine, and see how they come out. The world-mill is more complex than the calico-mill, and the architect stooped less. In the gingham-mill, a broken thread or a shred spoils the web through a piece of a hundred yards, and is traced back to the girl that wove it, and lessens her wages. The stockholder, on being shown this, rubs his hands with delight. Are you so cunning, Mr. Profitloss, and do you expect to swindle your master and employer, in the web you weave? A day is a more magnificent cloth than any muslin, the mechanism that makes it is infinitely cunninger, and you shall not conceal the sleezy, fraudulent, rotten hours you have slipped into the piece, nor fear that any honest thread, or straighter steel, or more inflexible shaft, will not testify in the web.

II. Wealth

As soon as a stranger is introduced into any company, one of the first questions which all wish to have answered, is, How does that man get his living? And with reason. He is no whole man until he knows how to earn a blameless livelihood. Society is barbarous, until every industrious man can get his living without dishonest customs.

Every man is a consumer, and ought to be a producer. He fails to make his place good in the world, unless he not only pays his debt, but also adds something to the common wealth. Nor can he do justice to his genius, without making some larger demand on the world than a bare subsistence. He is by constitution expensive, and needs to be rich.

Wealth has its source in applications of the mind to nature, from the rudest strokes of spade and axe, up to the last secrets of art. Intimate ties subsist between thought and all production; because a better order is equivalent to vast amounts of brute labor. The forces and the resistances are Nature's, but the mind acts in bringing things from where they abound to where they are wanted; in wise combining; in directing the practice of the useful arts, and in the creation of finer values, by fine art, by eloquence, by song, or the reproductions of memory. Wealth is in applications of mind to nature; and the art of getting rich consists not in industry, much less in saving, but in a better order, in timeliness, in being at the right spot. One man has stronger arms, or longer legs; another sees by the course of streams, and growth of markets, where land will be wanted, makes a clearing to the river, goes to sleep, wakes up rich. Steam is no stronger now, than it was a hundred years ago; but is put to better use. A clever fellow was acquainted with the expansive force of steam; he also saw the wealth of wheat and grass rotting in Michigan. Then he cunningly screws on the steam-pipe to the wheat-crop. Puff now, O Steam! The steam puffs and expands as before, but this time it is dragging all Michigan at its back to hungry New York and hungry England. Coal lay in ledges under the ground since the Flood, until a laborer with pick and windlass brings it to the surface. We may well call it black diamonds. Every basket is power and civilization. For coal is a portable climate. It carries the heat of the tropics to Labrador and the polar circle: and it is the means of transporting itself whithersoever it is wanted. Watt and Stephenson whispered in the ear of mankind their secret, that *a half-ounce of coal will draw two tons a mile*, and coal carries coal, by rail and by boat, to make Canada as warm as Calcutta, and with its comfort brings its industrial power.

When the farmer's peaches are taken from under the tree, and carried into town, they have a new look, and a hundredfold value over the fruit which grew on the same bough, and lies fulsomely on the ground. The craft of the merchant is this bringing a thing from where it abounds, to where it is costly.

Wealth begins in a tight roof that keeps the rain and wind out; in a good pump that yields you plenty of sweet water; in two suits of clothes, so to change your dress when you are wet; in dry sticks to burn; in a good double-wick lamp; and three meals; in a horse, or a locomotive, to cross the land; in a boat to cross the sea; in tools to work with; in books to read; and so, in giving, on all sides, by tools and auxiliaries, the greatest possible extension to our powers, as if it added feet, and hands, and eyes, and blood, length to the day, and knowledge, and good-will.

Wealth begins with these articles of necessity. And here we must recite the iron law which Nature thunders in these northern climates. First, she requires that each man should feed himself. If, happily, his fathers have left him no inheritance, he must go to work, and by making his wants less, or his gains more, he must draw himself out of that state of pain and insult in which she forces the beggar to lie. She gives him no rest until this is done: she starves, taunts, and torments him, takes away warmth, laughter, sleep, friends, and daylight, until he has fought his way to his own loaf. Then, less peremptorily, but still with sting enough, she urges him to the acquisition of such things as belong to him. Every warehouse and shop-window, every fruit-tree, every thought of every hour, opens a new want to him, which it concerns his power and dignity to gratify. It is of no use to argue the wants down: the philosophers have laid the greatness of man in making his wants few; but will a man content himself with a hut and a handful of dried pease? He is born to be rich. He is thoroughly related; and is tempted out by his appetites and fancies to the conquest of this and that piece of nature, until he finds his well-being in the use of his planet, and of more planets than his own. Wealth requires, besides the crust of bread and the roof,—the freedom of the city, the freedom of the earth, travelling, machinery, the benefits of science, music, and fine arts, the best culture, and the best company. He is the rich man who can avail himself of all men's faculties. He is the richest man who knows how to draw a benefit from the labors of the greatest number of men, of men in distant countries, and in past times. The same correspondence that is between thirst in the stomach, and water in the spring, exists between the whole of man and the whole of nature. The elements offer their service to him. The sea, washing the equator and the poles, offers its perilous aid, and the power and empire that follow it,—day by day to his craft and audacity. "Beware of me," it says, "but if you can hold me, I am the key to all the lands." Fire offers, on its side, an equal power. Fire, steam, lightning, gravity, ledges of rock, mines of iron, lead, quicksilver, tin, and gold; forests of all woods; fruits of all climates; animals of all habits; the powers of tillage; the fabrics of his chemic laboratory; the webs of his loom; the masculine draught of his locomotive, the talismans of the machine-shop; all grand and subtile things, minerals, gases, ethers, passions, war, trade, government, are his natural playmates, and, according to the excellence of the machinery in each human being, is his attraction for the instruments he is to employ. The world is his tool-chest, and he is successful, or his education is carried on just so far, as is the marriage of his faculties with nature, or, the degree in which he takes up things into himself.

The strong race is strong on these terms. The Saxons are the merchants of the world; now, for a thousand years, the leading race, and by nothing more than their quality of personal independence, and, in its special modification, pecuniary independence. No reliance for bread and games on the government, no clanship, no patriarchal style of living by the revenues of a chief, no marrying-on,—no system of clientship suits them; but every man must pay his scot. The English are prosperous and peaceable, with their habit of considering that every man must take care of himself, and has himself to thank, if he do not maintain and improve his position in society.

The subject of economy mixes itself with morals, inasmuch as it is a peremptory point of virtue that a man's independence be secured. Poverty demoralizes. A man in debt is so far a slave; and Wall-street thinks it easy for a millionaire to be a man of his word, a man of honor, but, that, in failing circumstances, no man can be relied on to keep his integrity. And when one observes in the hotels and palaces of our Atlantic capitals, the habit of expense, the riot of the senses, the absence of bonds, clanship, fellow-feeling of any kind, he feels, that, when a man or a woman is driven to the wall, the chances of integrity are frightfully diminished, as if virtue were coming to be a luxury which few could afford, or, as Burke said, "at a market almost too high for humanity." He may fix his inventory of necessities and of enjoyments on what scale he pleases, but if he wishes the power and privilege of thought, the chalking out his own career, and having society on his own terms, he must bring his wants within his proper power to satisfy.

The manly part is to do with might and main what you can do. The world is full of fops who never did anything, and who have persuaded beauties and men of genius to wear their fop livery, and these will deliver the fop opinion, that it is not respectable to be seen earning a living; that it is much more respectable to spend without earning; and this doctrine of the snake will come also from the elect sons of light; for wise men are not wise at all hours, and will speak five times from their taste or their humor, to once from their reason. The brave workman, who might betray his feeling of it in his manners, if he do not succumb in his practice, must replace the grace or elegance forfeited, by the merit of the work done. No matter whether he make shoes, or statues, or laws. It is the privilege of any human work which is well done to invest the doer with a certain haughtiness. He can well afford not to conciliate, whose faithful work will answer for him. The mechanic at his bench carries a quiet heart and assured manners, and deals on even terms with men of any condition. The artist has made his picture so true, that it disconcerts criticism. The statue is so beautiful, that it contracts no stain from the market, but makes the market a silent gallery for itself. The case of the young lawyer was pitiful to disgust,—a paltry matter of buttons or tweezer-cases; but the determined youth saw in it an aperture to insert his dangerous wedges, made the insignificance of the thing forgotten, and gave fame by his sense and energy to the name and affairs of the Tittleton snuffbox factory.

Society in large towns is babyish, and wealth is made a toy. The life of pleasure is so ostentatious, that a shallow observer must believe that this is the agreed best use of wealth, and, whatever is pretended, it ends in cosseting. But, if this were the main use of surplus capital, it would bring us to barricades, burned towns, and tomahawks, presently. Men of sense esteem wealth to be the assimilation of nature to themselves, the converting of the sap and juices of the planet to the incarnation and nutriment of their design. Power is what they want,—not candy;—power to execute their design, power to give legs and feet, form and actuality to their thought, which, to a clear-sighted man, appears the end for which the Universe exists, and all its resources might be well applied. Columbus thinks that the sphere is a problem for practical navigation, as well as for closet

geometry, and looks on all kings and peoples as cow-
ardly landsmen, until they dare fit him out. Few men
on the planet have more truly belonged to it. But he was
forced to leave much of his map blank. His successors
inherited his map, and inherited his fury to complete it.

So the men of the mine, telegraph, mill, map, and
survey,—the monomaniacs, who talk up their project
in marts, and offices, and entreat men to subscribe:—
how did our factories get built? how did North America
get netted with iron rails, except by the importunity of
these orators, who dragged all the prudent men in? Is
party the madness of many for the gain of a few? This
speculative genius is the madness of few for the gain of
the world. The projectors are sacrificed, but the public is the gainer. Each of these idealists, working after
his thought, would make it tyrannical, if he could. He
is met and antagonized by other speculators, as hot as
he. The equilibrium is preserved by these counterac-
tions, as one tree keeps down another in the forest, that
it may not absorb all the sap in the ground. And the
supply in nature of railroad presidents, copper-miners,
grand-junctioners, smoke-burners, fire-annihilators,
&c., is limited by the same law which keeps the propor-
tion in the supply of carbon, of alum, and of hydrogen.

To be rich is to have a ticket of admission to the
master-works and chief men of each race. It is to have

the sea, by voyaging; to visit the mountains, Niagara, the Nile, the desert, Rome, Paris, Constantinople; to see galleries, libraries, arsenals, manufactories. The reader of Humboldt's "Cosmos" follows the marches of a man whose eyes, ears, and mind are armed by all the science, arts, and implements which mankind have anywhere accumulated, and who is using these to add to the stock. So is it with Denon, Beckford, Belzoni, Wilkinson, Layard, Kane, Lepsius, and Livingston. "The rich man," says Saadi, "is everywhere expected and at home." The rich take up something more of the world into man's life. They include the country as well as the town, the ocean-side, the White Hills, the Far West, and the old European homesteads of man, in their notion of available material. The world is his, who has money to go over it. He arrives at the sea-shore, and a sumptuous ship has floored and carpeted for him the stormy Atlantic, and made it a luxurious hotel, amid the horrors of tempests. The Persians say, "'Tis the same to him who wears a shoe, as if the whole earth were covered with leather."

Kings are said to have long arms, but every man should have long arms, and should pluck his living, his instruments, his power, and his knowing, from the sun, moon, and stars. Is not then the demand to be rich legitimate? Yet, I have never seen a rich man. I have never seen a man as rich as all men ought to be, or, with an adequate command of nature. The pulpit and the press have many commonplaces denouncing the thirst for wealth; but if men should take these moralists at their word, and leave off aiming to be rich, the moralists would rush to rekindle at all hazards this love of power in the people, lest civilization should be undone. Men are urged by their ideas to acquire the command over nature. Ages derive a culture from the wealth of Roman Caesars, Leo Tenths, magnificent Kings of France, Grand Dukes of Tuscany, Dukes of Devonshire, Townleys, Vernons, and Peels, in England; or whatever great proprietors. It is the interest of all men, that there should be Vaticans and Louvres full of noble works of art; British Museums, and French Gardens of Plants, Philadelphia Academies of Natural History, Bodleian, Ambrosian, Royal, Congressional Libraries. It is the interest of all that there should be Exploring Expeditions; Captain Cooks to voyage round the world, Rosses, Franklins, Richardsons, and Kanes, to find the magnetic and the geographic poles. We are all richer for the measurement of a degree of latitude on the earth's surface. Our navigation is safer for the chart. How intimately our knowledge of the system of the Universe rests on that!—and a true economy in a state or an individual will forget its frugality in behalf of claims like these.

Whilst it is each man's interest, that, not only ease and convenience of living, but also wealth or surplus product should exist somewhere, it need not be in his hands. Often it is very undesirable to him. Goethe said well, "nobody should be rich but those who understand it." Some men are born to own, and can animate all their possessions. Others cannot: their owning is not graceful; seems to be a compromise of their character: they seem to steal their own dividends. They should own who can administer; not they who hoard and conceal; not they who, the greater proprietors they are, are only the greater beggars, but they whose work carves out work for more, opens a path for all. For he is the rich man in whom the people are rich, and he is the poor man in whom the people are poor: and how to give all access to the masterpieces of art and nature, is the problem of civilization. The socialism of our day has done good service in setting men on thinking how certain civilizing benefits, now only enjoyed by the opulent, can be enjoyed by all. For example, the providing to each man the means and apparatus of science, and of the arts. There are many articles good for occasional use, which few men are able to own. Every man wishes to see the ring of Saturn, the satellites and belts of Jupiter and Mars; the mountains and craters in the moon: yet how few can buy a telescope! and of those, scarcely one would like the trouble of keeping it in order, and exhibiting it. So of electrical and chemical apparatus, and many the like things. Every man may have occasion to consult books which he does not care to possess, such as cyclopaedias, dictionaries, tables, charts, maps, and public documents: pictures also of birds, beasts, fishes, shells, trees, flowers, whose names he desires to know.

There is a refining influence from the arts of Design on a prepared mind, which is as positive as that of music, and not to be supplied from any other source. But pictures, engravings, statues, and casts, beside their first cost, entail expenses, as of galleries and keepers for the exhibition; and the use which any man can make of them is rare, and their value, too, is much enhanced by the numbers of men who can share their enjoyment. In the Greek cities, it was reckoned profane, that any person should pretend a property in a work of art, which belonged to all who could behold it. I think sometimes,—could I only have music on my own terms;—could I live in a great city, and know where I could go whenever I wished the ablution and inundation of musical waves,—that were a bath and a medicine.

If properties of this kind were owned by states, towns, and lyceums, they would draw the bonds of neighborhood closer. A town would exist to an intellectual purpose. In Europe, where the feudal forms secure the permanence of wealth in certain families, those families buy and preserve these things, and lay them open to the public. But in America, where democratic institutions divide every estate into small portions, after a few years, the public should step into the place of these proprietors, and provide this culture and inspiration for the citizen.

Man was born to be rich, or, inevitably grows rich by the use of his faculties; by the union of thought with nature. Property is an intellectual production. The game requires coolness, right reasoning, promptness, and patience in the players. Cultivated labor drives out brute labor. An infinite number of shrewd men, in infinite years, have arrived at certain best and shortest ways of doing, and this accumulated skill in arts, cultures, harvestings, curings, manufactures, navigations, exchanges, constitutes the worth of our world to-day.

Commerce is a game of skill, which every man cannot play, which few men can play well. The right merchant is one who has the just average of faculties we call common sense; a man of a strong affinity for facts, who makes up his decision on what he has seen. He is thoroughly persuaded of the truths of arithmetic. There is always a reason, in the man, for his good or bad fortune, and so, in making money. Men talk as if there were some magic about this, and believe in magic, in all parts of life. He knows, that all goes on the old road, pound for pound, cent for cent,—for every effect a perfect cause,—and that good luck is another name for tenacity of purpose. He insures himself in every transaction, and likes small and sure gains. Probity and closeness to the facts are the basis, but the masters of the art add a certain long arithmetic. The problem is, to combine many and remote operations, with the accuracy and adherence to the facts, which is easy in near and small transactions; so to arrive at gigantic results, without any compromise of safety. Napoleon was fond of telling the story of the Marseilles banker, who said to his visitor, surprised at the contrast between the splendor of the banker's chateau and hospitality, and the meanness of the counting-room in which he had seen him,—"Young man, you are too young to understand how masses are formed,—the true and only power,—whether composed of money, water, or men, it is all alike,—a mass is an immense centre of motion, but it must be begun, it must be kept up:"—and he might have added, that the way in which it must be begun and kept up, is, by obedience to the law of particles.

Success consists in close appliance to the laws of the world, and, since those laws are intellectual and moral, an intellectual and moral obedience. Political Economy is as good a book wherein to read the life of man, and the ascendency of laws over all private and hostile influences, as any Bible which has come down to us.

Money is representative, and follows the nature and fortunes of the owner. The coin is a delicate meter of civil, social, and moral changes. The farmer is covetous of his dollar, and with reason. It is no waif to him. He knows how many strokes of labor it represents. His bones ache with the day's work that earned it. He knows how much land it represents;—how much rain, frost, and sunshine. He knows that, in the dollar, he gives you so much discretion and patience so much hoeing, and threshing. Try to lift his dollar; you must lift all that weight. In the city, where money follows the skit of a pen, or a lucky rise in exchange, it comes to be looked on as light. I wish the farmer held it dearer, and would spend it only for real bread; force for force.

The farmer's dollar is heavy, and the clerk's is light and nimble; leaps out of his pocket; jumps on to cards and faro-tables: but still more curious is its susceptibility to metaphysical changes. It is the finest barometer of social storms, and announces revolutions.

The value of a dollar is social, as it is created by society. Every man who removes into this city, with any purchasable talent or skill in him, gives to every man's labor in the city, a new worth. If a talent is anywhere born into the world, the community of nations is enriched; and, much more, with a new degree of probity. The expense of crime, one of the principal charges of every nation, is so far stopped. In Europe, crime is observed to increase or abate with the price of bread.

Wealth brings with it its own checks and balances. The basis of political economy is non-interference. The only safe rule is found in the self-adjusting meter of demand and supply. Do not legislate. Meddle, and you snap the sinews with your sumptuary laws. Give no bounties: make equal laws: secure life and property, and you need not give alms. Open the doors of opportunity to talent and virtue, and they will do themselves justice, and property will not be in bad hands. In a free and just commonwealth, property rushes from the idle and imbecile, to the industrious, brave, and persevering.

Our nature and genius force us to respect ends, whilst we use means. We must use the means, and yet, in our most accurate using, somehow screen and cloak them, as we can only give them any beauty, by a reflection of the glory of the end. That is the good head, which serves the end, and commands the means. The rabble are corrupted by their means: the means are too strong for them, and they desert their end.

1. The first of these measures is that each man's expense must proceed from his character. As long as your genius

buys, the investment is safe, though you spend like a monarch. Nature arms each man with some faculty which enables him to do easily some feat impossible to any other, and thus makes him necessary to society. This native determination guides his labor and his spending. He wants an equipment of means and tools proper to his talent. Do your work, respecting the excellence of the work, and not its acceptableness. Nothing is beneath you, if it is in the direction of your life: nothing is great or desirable, if it is off from that. I think we are entitled here to draw a straight line, and say, that society can never prosper, but must always be bankrupt, until every man does that which he was created to do.

Spend for your expense, and retrench the expense which is not yours. Allston, the painter, was wont to say, that he built a plain house, and filled it with plain furniture, because he would hold out no bribe to any to visit him, who had not similar tastes to his own. We are sympathetic, and, like children, want everything we see. But it is a large stride to independence,—when a man, in the discovery of his proper talent, has sunk the necessity for false expenses.

2. Spend after your genius, and by system. Nature goes by rule, not by sallies and saltations. There must be system in the economies. Saving and unexpensiveness

will not keep the most pathetic family from ruin, nor will bigger incomes make free spending safe. The secret of success lies never in the amount of money, but in the relation of income to outgo; as if, after expense has been fixed at a certain point, then new and steady rills of income, though never so small, being added, wealth begins.

3. The rule is not to dictate, nor to insist on carrying out each of your schemes by ignorant wilfulness, but to learn practically the secret spoken from all nature, that things themselves refuse to be mismanaged, and will show to the watchful their own law. Nobody need stir hand or foot. The custom of the country will do it all. I know not how to build or to plant; neither how to buy wood, nor what to do with the house-lot, the field, or the wood-lot, when bought. Never fear: it is all settled how it shall be, long beforehand, in the custom of the country, whether to sand, or whether to clay it, when to plough, and how to dress, whether to grass, or to corn; and you cannot help or hinder it. Nature has her own best mode of doing each thing, and she has somewhere told it plainly, if we will keep our eyes and ears open.

4. Another point of economy is to look for seed of the same kind as you sow: and not to hope to buy one kind

with another kind. Friendship buys friendship; justice; justice; military merit, military success. Good husbandry finds wife, children, and household. The good merchant large gains, ships, stocks, and money. The good poet fame, and literary credit; but not either, the other. Yet there is commonly a confusion of expectations on these points. Hotspur lives for the moment; praises himself for it; and despises Furlong, that he does not. Hotspur, of course, is poor; and Furlong a good provider. The odd circumstance is, that Hotspur thinks it a superiority in himself, this improvidence, which ought to be rewarded with Furlong's lands.

5. Now these things are so in Nature. All things ascend, and the royal rule of economy is, that it should ascend also, or, whatever we do must always have a higher aim. Thus it is a maxim, that money is another kind of blood. So there is no maxim of the merchant, e.g., "Best use of money is to pay debts;" "Every business by itself;" "Best time is present time;" "The right investment is in tools of your trade;" or the like, which does not admit of an extended sense. The counting-room maxims liberally expounded are laws of the Universe. The merchant's economy is a coarse symbol of the soul's economy. It is, to spend for power, and

not for pleasure. It is to invest income; that is to say, to take up particulars into generals; days into integral eras,—literary, emotive, practical, of its life, and still to ascend in its investment. The merchant has but one rule, absorb and invest: he is to be capitalist: the scraps and filings must be gathered back into the crucible; the gas and smoke must be burned, and earnings must not go to increase expense, but to capital again. Well, the man must be capitalist. Will he spend his income, or will he invest? His body and every organ is under the same law. His body is a jar, in which the liquor of life is stored. Will he spend for pleasure? The way to ruin is short and facile. Will he not spend, but hoard for power? It passes through the sacred fermentations, by that law of Nature whereby everything climbs to higher platforms, and bodily vigor becomes mental and moral vigor. The bread he eats is first strength and animal spirits: it becomes, in higher laboratories, imagery and thought; and in still higher results, courage and endurance. This is the right compound interest; this is capital doubled, quadrupled, centupled; man raised to his highest power.

The true thrift is always to spend on the higher plane; to invest and invest, with keener avarice, that he may spend in spiritual creation, and not in augmenting animal existence. Nor is the man enriched, in repeating the old experiments of animal sensation, nor unless through new powers and ascending pleasures, he knows himself by the actual experience of higher good, to be already on the way to the highest.

Born in 1803 in Boston, Massachusetts, RALPH WALDO EMERSON was one of America's preeminent men of letters. The inspiration for the school of philosophy called Transcendentalism, Emerson, in his essays, journals, lectures, and letters, traced out a view of life that located man as an extension and reflection of the Divine, owing his existence and allegiance to none but the highest insights of his own nature. An inspiration on figures ranging from his contemporary Henry David Thoreau to William James, Emerson formulated what can be called the American spiritual vision: non-dogmatic, nonsectarian, and based in the integrity and primacy of the individual spiritual search. In that sense, Emerson is also the founding figure of much of the modern spiritual culture in the West. After many years as a writer, publisher, lecturer, and seeker, he died in 1882 in Concord, Massachusetts, where his house still stands today.

MITCH HOROWITZ is the PEN Award-winning author of books including *Occult America* and *The Miracle Club*. A writer-in-residence at the New York Public Library and lecturer-in-residence at the University of

Philosophical Research in Los Angeles, Mitch introduces and edits G&D Media's line of Condensed Classics and is the author of the Napoleon Hill Success Course series, including *The Miracle of a Definite Chief Aim* and *The Power of the Master Mind*. Visit him at MitchHorowitz.com.

Printed in the USA
CPSIA information can be obtained
at www.ICGtesting.com
JSHW012046140824
68134JS00034B/3288

9 781722 501983